Why I Joined the United Nations Association Student Chapter

The United Nations Millennium and Sustainable Development Goals

You can change the world by joining too!

Why I Joined the United Nations Association Student Chapter

The United Nations Millennium and Sustainable Development Goals

You can change the world by joining too!

By

Dr. LaVonne Downey

Dr. Monique Herard

Contributors

Kenia Marreros

Sharon Darrow

Paul Dismukes

Denise Cahue

Lashondra Graves

Gary Baker

Rachel Dalton

Blessing Jaja

Mary Lorraine Andoh

Eric Kelley

Editors

Dr. La Vonne Downey

Dr. Monique Herard

Lashondra Graves, MBA

lgme

Printed in the United States of America
First Printing, 2015
 ISBN 978-1-329-17806-9

First Printing, 2015

ISBN 978-1-329-17806-9

Published   by   Lashondra   Graves   Marketing   Enterprizes   (LGME)

lgme

7344 South Shore Drive
Chicago IL,
60649
www.lgmarketingenterprizes.com

Special discounts are available on quantity purchases by corporations, associations, educators and others. For details, contact the publisher at above listed address.

U.S. trade bookstores and wholesalers: Please contact Lashondra Graves Marketing   Enterprizes   at   (773)-308-8632   or customerservice@lgmarketingenterprizes.com

Please Contact the Authors if you are a UNA Student Chapter or any UNA Chapter to learn how you can use this book for fundraisers. You can contact each Author here:
Dr. LaVonne Downey- ldowney@roosevelt.edu
Dr. Monique Herard- mherard@robertmorris.edu

Dedication

This book is dedicated to all the future members of the United Nations Association Student Chapters. Together we can make a change in the world, one determined Student at a time!

Find out if your University Chapter and if it doesn't contact the United Nations Associaton to find out how you can get a chapter started in your school.

Contact the UNA-USA at unausa.org

"We have the know-how and the means to address these challenges, but we need urgent leadership and joint action now". "These are universal challenges. They demand new levels of multilateral action, based on evidence and built on shared values, principles and priorities for a common   destiny."

"The stars are aligned for the world to take historic action to transform lives and protect the planet. I urge Governments and people everywhere to fulfill their political and moral responsibilities. This is my call to dignity, and we must respond with all our vision and strength," **Ban Ki Moon-United Nations Secretary General**

Table of Contents

Acknowledgements

We would like to thank all our teachers- present and past, my editor, creative writing course classmates, and our families without whose help this book would never have been completed.

Thank you for your patience and guidance, your use of the editor's red pen...

We would also like to thank the United Nations Association, the United Nations Association-Chicago, and its board members for encouraging a new generation of responsible global citizens.

Introduction

What connects us to an idea, each other, and the world is as varied and as numerous as the stars. Some of us are attracted to big overarching concepts whereas others of us by a singular personal experience. These varieties of reasons are what can be seen in this book. It shows how the Millennium Development Goals (MDG) and the Sustainable Development Goals (SDG) are linked and why these students and their faculty advisers joined and became active in their campus United Nations Association. Although there are sometimes similarities in the goals chosen they express themselves to each member in differing ways. After reading them you will see many examples of how an organization with a wide array of goals and focus can attract and bring together articulate involved individuals that use their expanse of talents to work towards a greater good, beyond state and national lines.

The book also contains a brief history of the goals. This was done not so much to educate the reader but to show that there are threads in their inception, execution, and subsequent expansion from the MDG to the proposed SDG. These threads are also present in the individual essays about them contained in this book. The first thread is the identification of oneself as a global citizen. This means they view the world as interdependent. This is often expressed as a mutual dependence through economic, social, and or interpersonal reliance and responsibility to each other. This creates a global view in which the world is viewed as a system in which individual, societies, global actors, and nation's behaviors affect the entire system.

The second thread is social justice, which means that society should be fair, with a reciprocal obligation to ensure that all people regardless of race, social class, gender and sexual orientation should have equal access to succeed in life. There is an acceptance and expectation of diversity. Diversity that respects and understands that each individual is unique, important and equal despite race, gender, sexual orientation, ethnicity, age, physical abilities, religious beliefs and ideologies. All of this is built upon an idea of human rights. Human rights which are inherent and belong to all people regardless of nationality, sex, religion, race or any other human characteristic.

Although these all seem as though they are lofty concepts, they are artfully present in the individual essays and in each University's chapter of the United Nations Association. They show that there are many ways to view the MDGs but also the mission of the United Nations. This book, its contents and the University United Nations Associations chapters are all examples of the tenant that Dag Hammerskjold, one of the first Secretary Generals of the UN, when he said that "when people, just people, stop thinking of the United Nations as a weird Picasso abstraction and see it as a drawing they made themselves is when it will flourish." This is what these students decided to do and this book depicts that drawing they made themselves!

The United Nations Association's Millennium Development Goals

The 8 Millennium Development Goals

1 — ERADICATE EXTREME POVERTY AND HUNGER

2 — ACHIEVE UNIVERSAL PRIMARY EDUCATION

3 — PROMOTE GENDER EQUALITY AND EMPOWER WOMEN

4 — REDUCE CHILD MORTALITY

5 — IMPROVE MATERNAL HEALTH

6 — COMBAT HIV/AIDS, MALARIA AND OTHER DISEASES

7 — ENSURE ENVIRONMENTAL SUSTAINABILITY

8 — GLOBAL PARTNERSHIP FOR DEVELOPMENT

This book is a compilation of the United Nations Association - USA Student Chapters. The contributors give their experience as student members. They tell you, from their perspectives, how the UNA-USA Student Chapters have personally affected their lives as students and professionals! The writers of this book use the UN's Millennium Development Goals and the Sustainable Development Goals to show you how powerful the UNA is in the world.

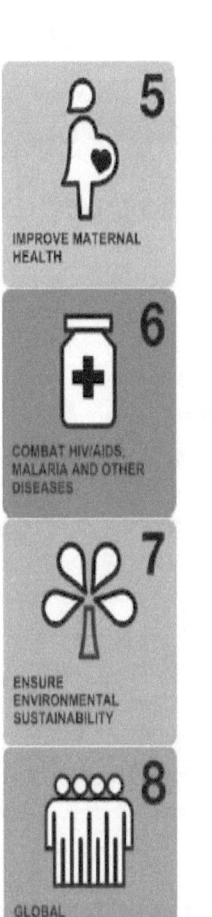

Goal 1: Eradicate extreme poverty and hunger

Goal 2: Achieve universal primary education

Goal 3: Promote gender equality and empower women

Goal 4: Reduce child mortality

Goal 5: Improve maternal health

Goal 6: Combat HIV/AIDS, malaria and other diseases

Goal 7: Ensure environmental sustainability

Goal 8: Develop a Global Partnership for Development

Meet Our Faculty Advisors for the Robert Morris University and Roosevelt University's Student UNA-USA Chapters!

Dr. La Vonne Downey is associate professor of Health Services/ Public Administration at Roosevelt University where it is her honor to teach the brightest, most innovative, involved and compassionate students. She teaches medical ethics, health policy, global health policy, health economics, integrated health systems, health marketing, congressional policy making, research methods and evaluation, statistics, and the capstone course for Public Administration. She has authored or co-authored over 75 articles on a range of topics such as: identifying and solving health (medicine and psychiatric) care issues at the local, national and international level; preventive healthcare; medical education; violence prevention; access and cost and payment of care; and effects of changes on standards of care, especially for underserved. She is currently a member of Editorial boards of the Journal of Hospital Administration, Journal of International Emergency Medicine, and Journal of Dataset in Papers in Medicine, as well as a reviewer for several medical and public health journals. Additionally, she was a former Model UN student, UNA Board member and currently the chair of International Health initiatives for UNA Chicago and the faculty advisor for Roosevelt University United Nations Student Organization

The thread of health ties together the Millennium goals. The Millennium Goals force us to look at and understand the role of health in a different way. In examining them in this manner one can see that they are all inter- connected. The role of improving health in one goal creates a domino effect that imparts change in the seven others.

In order to improve maternal health (goal 5) and reduce child mortality (goal 4) efforts must be made to eradicate extreme poverty and hunger (goal 1), as women and children make up the highest percentage 60 % of those living in poverty and hunger. Subsequently 50 % of pregnant women in developing countries lack proper nutrition, resulting in 240,000 maternal deaths and one out of every six infants being born with a low birth weight. As of 2011,

6.9 million children died each year from preventable health issues such as malaria, measles, and pneumonia this falls into preventing disease (goal 6). Efforts to combat disease through universal immunization, as of 2014, have reduced child mortality by 50% (goal 4). None of this would have been possible without a global partnership with Shot At Life, GAVI, Gates Foundation, and Rotary International, all of whom developed and distributed vaccines via community based health workers. Thus these global partnerships for development (goal 8) produced a cadre of local community health centers run by and for the communities.

Giving everyone access to primary education (goal 2) means a healthier population overall as educational levels are directly related to health outcomes. Educating women in particularly has a multiplier effect on health. For every year beyond primary education that women receive there is a 12% reduction in infant and child mortality. An educated woman is more likely to educate their own children. It has also been shown that increasing in household income reduced child mortality risk. This impact is 20 times larger if the income is from the mother versus the father (goal 3). According to the International Monetary Fund educating women can impact countries GDP within 9 to 30% increase with a sustainable impact of 4%, thus impacting overall poverty levels.

Promotion of sustainable development (goal 7) impacts the safety and reliability of water and food resources. Currently, 2.3 billion people suffer from water-borne diseases each year. However, with access to clean water and diverse food resources there will be a reduction in child hood mortality, improved maternal health and reduction in the number of water borne diseases such as cholera.

In 2012, a total of 7 million deaths were related to air pollution with women and children being at particular risk. Air pollutions are often related to non sustainable policies in transportation, energy, manufacturing and waste disposal. A more health related strategy towards development will be more economical in part due to health-care cost savings as well as environmental sustainability gains.

A thread of health ties together the Millennium Goals. Thus understanding these eight goals and the way that health connects them can help move us from an isolated concept of self, outward to a responsibility and connection that spills over borders and into a world community. As Kant says all humans have absolute worth simply by the act of their existence and my health and all that impacts it matters, as does everyone else's, no matter where they live. ~Dr. Downey

Dr. Monique Herard is a Professor of Management at Robert Morris University- Illinois. Dr. Herard teaches principles of management, management information systems, business ethics, organizational behavior, program and curriculum administration and assessment. She has published and presented in the areas of online education, student achievement, and assessment in higher education, and served as a reviewer for several publications relating to information systems.

Dr. Herard is also the faculty advisor for the UNA-USA at RMU student organization. She served on the Board of UNA-USA Greater Chicago Chapter and is currently the Under-Secretary General of Education for InterGenMUN - UNA Chicago. She speaks three languages and is a member of the Chicago Council on Global Affairs and the Alliance Française of Chicago.

I acknowledge that all of the Millennium Development Goals (MDGs') are important. However, I am particularly drawn to MDG #2, "Achieve universal primary education." For me, education is the foundation for upward mobility and the bedrock upon which the other MDG goals lie. A case in point, if all students in low income countries left school with basic reading skills, there could be a 12% cut in global poverty. This equates to 171 million people being lifted out of poverty (Education for All Global Monitoring Report, 2011). Education, of all the goals, is a prerequisite for long term economic growth and is a crucial building block for an inclusive, democratic society (Pegg, 2013). As countries become more interconnected globally the need for educated citizens, citizens with the requisite academic and life skills to contribute constructively to society, becomes critical.

The MDGs were adopted in September 2000 at the Millennium Summit. Since then, there has been some progress toward universal primary education. For example, developing regions saw a 7% increase (83% in 2000 to 90% in 2012) in their adjusted net enrollment rate for primary education. The youth literacy rate for the population 15–24 years old increased globally, from 83 per cent in 1990 to 89 per cent in 2012. The adult literacy rate, for the population 15 years and older, increased from 76 per cent to 84 per cent. Three regions Northern Africa, Southern Asia, and Oceania have already met their millennium development target goals for 2015 (Millennium Development Goals: 2014 Progress Chart, 2014).

While these gains are noteworthy, much more is needed to achieve universal primary education. Some of the challenges to achieving this goal have been (1) continued increase in the dropout rate, (2) the number of illiterates remains high; 781 million adults and 126 million youth worldwide lacked basic reading and writing skills in 2012, (3) continued disparities in school attendance linked to gender, poverty, place of residence, and disabilities, and (4) donors have not fulfilled the promise made in 2000 that " no countries would be left behind due to lack of resources." Low income countries, who rely on aid to basic education, have been impacted the most. Their aid fell by 9 per cent between 2010 and 2011, from $2.1 billion to $1.9 billion (Millennium Development Goals: 2014

Progress Chart, 2014). Without adequate resources and support, low income countries cannot maintain the infrastructure necessary for sustainable improvements toward universal primary education. The United Nations Association of the United States of America (UNA-USA), through its advocacy agenda, is in a unique position to ensure that the U.S. continues to support and pay its fair share of international funding to achieve the eight MDG's.

UNA-USA is an "organization dedicated to inform, inspire, and mobilize the American people to support the ideals and vital work of the United Nations,"(unausa.org). My role as an advisor is to mentor and support my student members of UNA-USA to become informed global citizens who strive to make a difference. The U.S. Fund for UNICEF defines a global citizen as "someone who understands global interdependence, respects and values diversity, has the ability to challenge injustice and inequities and takes action in a way that is personally meaningful." A global citizen is also an educated citizen. Therefore, education is a requisite for participation in global discourse. My students have the requisite for participation. However, many around the world do not. As indicated earlier, there are millions of adults and youths who lack basic reading and writing skills. These fundamental academic skills are tools of empowerment and hope for millions. Each global citizen has a responsibility to ensure that these skills are attained by 2030. Inclusive and equitable quality education for all by 2030 is an achievable goal that will likely reduce the information asymmetry that currently exists and create a path of opportunities for those who aspire to contribute constructively to society. What an intriguing world it would be if all were afforded the right to a quality education!

Dr. Monique Herard

THERE'S STILL
MUCH TO DO

GOAL 1

Eradicate Extreme Hunger and Poverty

Kenai Marreros *is a student at Robert Morris University, currently working towards a Bachelor's degree in Business Management. Upon graduation, she will become the first person in her family to graduate from college. She plans to put her knowledge to use in a company that aims to help make this world a better place, one person at a time. She also wants to create a foundation that reuses books and school supplies to send to other students living in less developed countries, who do not receive support for their education but challenge their circumstances and inspire her every day to continue her education.*

Eradicate Extreme Poverty

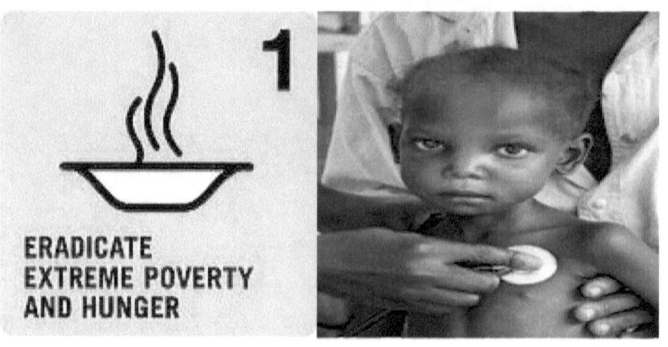

ERADICATE EXTREME POVERTY AND HUNGER

As I tried to finish my plate of food, I glanced across the table I and saw a plate with a handful of fries and two untouched chicken wings that were to be directed straight to a garbage can without the hope of ever being savored. I was appalled and outraged by this sighting as I knew "there are many kids in Africa who have nothing to eat," a common phrase among those trying to innate guilt for wasting food, but it was not my first nor will it be my last sight of discarded food.

According to the United Nations, "globally, about 842 million people are estimated to be undernourished." Millions of people, ranging from babies, to teens, to elders. Pause and repeat that fact again. It is astonishing to think that in this age as I struggle to gather $5 for a Subway, others struggle for even a piece of bread.

As I await impatiently for dinner because I missed breakfast this morning, others have to wait for dinner, breakfast, lunch, and next day's dinner in order to eat. Unlike me, though, missing breakfast was not of their choice, but to a lack of food. While we indulge in Panera, Wingstop, Panda Express and other foods, kids around the world are scrambling to find a speckle of food to calm their hunger. These starving kids amount to "more than 99 million children under age five who are still undernourished and underweight." Therefore, as the more fortunate people that we are, in comparison to them, we should not only advocate for them but also initiate a change where the number of millions of children starving can be reduced to thousands.

How is it that we can be appalled and argue with rage at hearing parents starving their kids in the U.S, when there are millions of kids around the world going unnoticed for the same reason? It is injustices like this that aroused my interest to join the United Nations Association-USA. Through their proposed sustainable development goals, I felt that I could make a difference and reach out to others who share the same passions, like "ending hunger, achieving food security and improve nutrition, and promote sustainable agriculture" (UNA-USA proposed 17 sustainable development goals).Uniting to help a cause like this can bring us a feeling of fulfillment and hope for a better future for us and the ones who need it. These adults and kids need us with the same urgency that our body needs food.

Sharon C. Darrow is a full-time student and tea-barista who can't seem to stop moving towards various goals. She is an Accounting Major at Robert Morris University, but has a background education that leads toward Chemistry and Sociology. Too much positive energy and a thirst for knowledge, means she is on a never ending goal to make the world a better place. During the spring of 2015 she became the secretary to UNA-USA's RMU chapter.

There are many types of people in the world. However, I feel as though there are two major attitudes toward making a change in the world, and it equates to positive and negative. I find myself to be the former and wanting to be a part of change. Before finding this organization, I had very little ideas on how to participate beyond what little I currently do; whether it is promoting gender positivity in my friend's son, by making sure he knew he could play as

Wonder Woman, or telling my friends to vote even during Mid-term elections. These ultimately are small things, but my hope is making a greater impact later on. While I have a positive attitude about my current actions, I still feel there is more I can do.

At UNA-USA I found a set of goals that I didn't even know the UN was striving for. The overall theme is obviously making everyone's lives better globally, the two that stick out to me the most though are: "End Poverty in all its forms everywhere" and "Achieve gender equality and empower all women and girls." The latter is an obvious choice to me, since I am feminist. The first, though, is something I have always wanted to devote more of my time to, but as an adult, I didn't know where to start..

In my Catholic grade school, we used to do donation Friday's, which meant if you donated a dollar you got to wear Jeans to school and the money would go to a charity. My personal favorite thought was raising money for bicycles, for children in India. My math teacher was in contact with a missionary from India, and he would write to her and others for donations to the school that would help get supplies and bicycles for the kids. After the kids hit a certain age, they would have to go the next village to further their education, and it was a little over an hour walk or a 15 minute bike ride. So the missionary had the idea to get bicycles for them to drastically cut the commute time. Whenever there was enough money to purchase another bicycle, they would send us a photo of the new bike(s). We managed to raise enough in a school year for five bicycles, and the excitement from the photos was a pretty awesome feeling to know you had an impact on the other side of the globe.

The reason I spent time on that story is because I personally feel there are ways of helping people if we give them the tools to succeed. Whether its bikes to get you to another school or money for nets that can help prevent malaria, these are little steps that make not only someone's day but their livelihood as well. Today's world is no longer just local, our communities are now global. We need to have compassion and aid those who need help, because one never knows when one will need the same.

While I do want to focus my time on global efforts, I also feel just as passionate about making a difference for the people in my city. Chicago is the major city of the Midwest, and being a big liberal city attracts a lot of youths. Through UNA-USA, I believe, I and others can be a part of making a difference both locally and globally. If we all put our efforts toward helping someone today, it will improve everyone's world tomorrow.

GOAL 2

Acheiving Universal Primary Education

Paul Dismukes *recently graduated from Roosevelt University with an MPA degree with a concentration Health Care Services. He received his B.A. in Political Science with a concentration in International Relations from the University of Illinois at Chicago. Additionally, he is an 11-year navy veteran and has extensive public service experience at both the state and federal levels. He will be continuing his studies and is going to Brandeis University to earn a doctorate degree in Health Policy and eventually work for either the United Nations or the European Union on global health initiatives. His future goals were one of the reasons he joined the UNA-USA Student Chapter at Roosevelt University. Being a member of the student chapter has been very enriching. The UNA-USA Millennial Goal that stood out for him was* ***#2 Achieving Universal Primary Education!***

Achieve Universal Primary Education

ACHIEVE UNIVERSAL
PRIMARY EDUCATION

In September 2000, the United Nations signed the Millennium Declaration, which commits UN member states to combat poverty, hunger, disease, illiteracy, environmental degradation, and discrimination against women. The 191 UN member states have agreed to try to achieve these Millennium Development Goals (MDGs) within this calendar year. For universal primary education in particular, the aim is to "ensure that, by 2015, children everywhere, boys and girls alike, will be able to complete a full course of primary schooling."i In light of the varying degrees of civil war, economic instability, and political strife within countries, achieving this goal may prove challenging especially because it is fashioned to run concurrently, as opposed to before, these other development goals. In this commentary, I argue the case for achieving universal primary education as the necessary first step, with a few safeguards attached, because it underlies the success of the other seven MDGs.

Think of it this way: if you are a Chicago resident and your car fails to start on one of our finger-numbing February mornings, then it's a good chance that your battery has died. However, this is no guarantee and a lot depends on your car's history and your own level of mechanical expertise. In order to fix the problem you could spend a portion or all of your limited resources on a car battery, an alternator, and/or an alley mechanic (in Chicago every neighborhood has one) to troubleshoot the car's electrical system. While this is an over-simplification of the challenges with the MDGs, it nevertheless illustrates the point that I would like to make. Instead of one conclusion (car won't start), the United

Nations sees several and therefore addresses each one with a required response. However this may be an over-complication in impoverished communities in much the same way that a hungry person needing food cares about operationalizing terms such as balanced diet and low sugar intake. In this hypothetical scenario, would it be effective to satisfy her hunger by shoving a serving of steak, broccoli and bread into her mouth at the same time and expecting her to chew it all down in a single sitting, with a less than desired inside knowledge about her bodily makeup and even less of a history with her? Or is it more feasible to allow her, at her own leisure, to eat a sufficient amount of protein, then some carbohydrates, and then a conservative amount of fat? More importantly, universal primary education should not be considered one of these servings, but rather the plate upon which the other agenda items are carried to the table.

Several arguments can be made for achieving universal primary education first. Economically, global interdependence rewards countries that discover their niches in the market and early level education and training increases the chances that children grow into innovative and productive citizens. Politically, formal education starts citizens on the track of information gathering and deductive reasoning—tools necessary for selecting better elected officials (in democracies) and for positive regime change over time. Herbert Spencer once said, "The great aim of education is not knowledge, but action". Socially, formal education helps teach children structure and makes them less prone to violence. Finally, universal formal education could indirectly address the UN's other MDGs such as gender inequality, maternity deaths and hunger as evidenced by the World Food Programme's (WFP) Food For Girls' Education Programme that has been tackling hunger and enrollment challenges in Yemen.

With that said, there should be some safeguards in place for the universal primary education goal to exceed expectations. First, consideration must be given to whether the teachings come from within a particular country or from outside of the country. This matters for two reasons: 1) if primary education is taught at a remote location, then transportation and the communication of infectious disease are a concern and 2) if the teaching is done on the outside, then the language in which the education is being taught will likely be foreign to the students. In countries like South Asia and sub-Saharan Africa, where the educational need is the greatest and dialects are often unique to groups within these groups, outside teaching could prove challenging. Second, a universal primary education plan, whether conducted locally or remotely, will require a great deal of resources. Finally, the United Nations would have to get some regimes to set aside their gender biases and admit as many female students to the program as male students. While this task appears simple and quite evident, many regimes have bigoted beliefs that have only been reinforced over time. These challenges can be safeguarded with an inclusion of the home country in the educational plan, partnering with numerous nonprofit entities aimed at similar outcomes (i.e. Save the Children, UNICEF), and strong political advocacy within the United Nations, European Union, and other international organizations.

Because I believe that these safeguards can be instituted by the United Nations and the success of the other MDGs can be multiplied with the establishment of universal primary education, the second stated goal really needs to be the organization's first.

Denise Cahue *recently earned her Bachelor's of Business Administration with a concentration in Management and Finance from Robert Morris University. She was Robert Morris University's Spring 2015 commencement speaker. While at Robert Morris, she served as President of the Tau Sigma-Gamma Omega college chapter. She became a member of Robert Morris University's UNA chapter by representing the chapter as its public relations intern through securing partnerships with local businesses and promoting club fundraising events. She is a first generation college graduate, who places an e great emphasis on life-long learning. Therefore, she plans to give back to the community by assisting and mentoring those in need of guidance through the process of attaining a higher education. This is why the Millennial Goal that spoke to her was* **#2 Achieving Universal Primary Education!**

Achieving Universal Primary Education

Scrolling through social media, I came across the quote, "What if the cure for Cancer was trapped inside the mind of someone who can't afford an education." As a college senior weeks away from receiving her Bachelors degree, it caused me to stop and think about my own education. I have always valued education as a life-long process; I never considered not furthering my education as an option. I even viewed college as an absolute. Yes, college is expensive, but I was determined to earn my degree and establish a career for myself. I attended community college for two years and then transferred to Robert Morris University. I earned scholarships and I took out loans, knowing that the hard work I put into my education would be worth it. I majored in Business Administration with a concentration in Management and a second concentration in Finance. Yet, this quote put education into a worldly perspective.

It is truly a terrifying thought. Everyone has the potential to make an impact on the world; however, that potential many times is not realized due to inaccessible, inequitable, poor quality education.

Many people in developing countries either cannot afford an education or cannot attain an education due to culturally established gender inequalities. Previously represented by the second Millennium Development Goal in achieving universal primary education established in the year 2000, the newly founded sustainable development goal addressing education aims to take things a few steps further. Through the United Nations' sustainable development goal (number four) of ensuring inclusive and equitable quality education and promoting life-long learning opportunities for all, we can aim to change all that by the year 2030.

Globally, the goal is for all boys and girls to complete primary and secondary education. This includes access to early childhood development in preparing children for primary education. By 2030, we also want all youth to achieve literacy, as well as, numeracy. Furthermore, we will reach equal access to education at all levels, including at the university level, for all men and women, including those with disabilities. This objective will be realized through the building and upgrading of education facilities that provide safe, inclusive, and effective learning environments. In addition, qualified teachers are necessary to provide the proper education. Qualified teachers will be made available through international cooperation in teacher training in developing countries. Students, however, still need to be able to afford an education. Therefore, more scholarships will be made available to students in developing countries in order to obtain a higher education whether it is in other developing countries or developed countries.

Beyond attaining a higher education, we wish to increase the number of youth and adults who have the necessary skills to acquire decent employment and entrepreneurships, as well as, further promote sustainable development education, lifestyles, human rights, gender equality, a culture of peace, global citizenship, and an appreciation for cultural diversity and the contribution to sustainable development.

Education is a powerful thing. The country we were born in, our gender, our status, or our ability to pay for it should not determine whether or not we get an education. Everyone should have access to an enriching education and to the possibility of making a global difference.

GOAL 3

Promote Gender Equality and
Empower Women

Lashondra Graves! Is a *member of the Robert Morris University of Illinois United Nations Association Student Chapter. She has a B.A. and M.B.A. in Management, both from Robert Morris University of Illinois. She is currently an Adjunct Faculty member at Robert Morris University of Illinois and owns a full service Social Media and Internet Marketing/Advertising Firm, LGME-Lashondra Graves Marketing Enterprizes. She also published her first book last year titled, Chasing Signs. She has an International Ministry entitled To the Least of These. Her ministry has so far partnered with Agape Ministry located in Kakinada India and Christ Glory Ministry located in Pakistan. Her goal is to reach the world by whatever means necessary, thus her full service advertising and marketing firm. She knows that every 1 adds up, literally everyone adds up and for everyone (1) that stands up, we will have change! The goal that stood out for her was **#3 Promote Gender Equality and Empower Women.***

Promote Gender Equality and Empower Women

When people hear promote gender equality in the U.S, the first thing that comes to mind is equal pay, equal jobs etc, but this Millennial Development Goal goes deeper. Yes, the equal employment issue is at the top of the list because it's easier seen and is a problem all over the world.

In the Worldwide Government Sector only 7 of the highest 150 elected heads of state are women and only 11 of 192 heads of government positions are held by women.

If you look at Forbes rich list, most of the women on the list are from rich families or are executive's at large businesses such as Wal-Mart, Apple or IBM. To go even further, there are fewer than 25 women Chief Executive Officers in the 500 largest corporations in America, making that less than 5%!

A story published in "the Guardian" stated that in the 27 member countries of the European Union (EU) women accounted for only 16.6% of board members of large publicly listed companies.

This is a widely spread problem across the world, but as I stated before it's the most talked about problem because it's easier seen and the data can't be hidden.

Underneath this problem comes lack of proper education. There are countries that still don't afford women the same educational rights as men. You would think this wasn't true, especially since women are the ones raising the children. With the single family household structures on the rise All Over the World with vast majority of them having the mother as the head of the household, you can see how the gender equality issue can have a domino effect on the world.

A story published in "the Huffington Post" stated that Single-mother families in poverty increased for the fourth straight year to 4.1 million, or 41.5 percent. This was only in the United States in 2013. The story goes on to say and I quote "Many of these mothers are low income with low education. " Do you see a problem here? Most of these mothers are low income with low education.

But wait, the education inequality is the second biggest issue talked about because like job inequality it's hard to hide and the information is readily available. What this means is there are other issues underneath this one.

Issues such as violence against women, sexual slavery and so on.

When I think of gender equality I don't look at it as "make the woman the head of a 'Cooperative Family Structure" or rather two parent family structure, because there is a natural order and I respect that natural order. However; when you live in a world where the families are split up and having one parent in a household becomes a norm, a world where the law makes it easy for men to leave a household or have more than one; you have to adjust. This adjustment is going to take Gender Equality. Think about it, without Gender Equality rising up to meet the new world standards, the gap between who can have big jobs and who can't is going to get bigger, because it is the Mothers teaching the children including their male children in these new norms and they can only give them what they have. I want to leave you with this, under bigger publicized issues there are always smaller worst issues springing up and unfortunately for women these smaller issues includes heinous crimes against a human being.

MDG 4

Reduce Child Mortality

Gary Baker is an undergraduate student at Robert Morris University studying Business Accounting. He is a currently a senior completing his final quarter before his degree. After graduation, Gary will continue his education on master's level where he plans to study further in the field of accounting.

Afterwards he would like to join the Peace Corps and give back to the community. His motto in life is that "where there is no struggle, there is no strength." every day is a blessing and should be lived to the fullest

Reduce Child Mortality

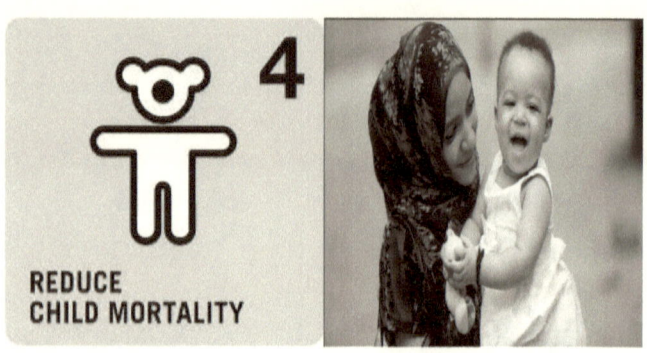

REDUCE CHILD MORTALITY

Take a moment and think of the word "family" and what it means to you. The joy or frustration that compels you due to your family or lack their of. There are times where family is everything to us and times also where we get annoyed by them, more specifically our parents. Our mother and father are the two sole individuals that give us life. Think of your childhood and how you were raised, the happy moments where you asked yourself, "What would I do without them?" We never asked ourselves, "What would they do without us?"

My mother once told me the greatest moment of her life was the moment I was born, when she held me in her arms. She told me from that moment on she knew she would never be lonely again. I later found out that my birth meant so much to her because I was the only child of hers that made it. Prior to my birth she had two premature deliveries. She explained to me the hurt and the pain of creating something so beautiful only to never be able to watch it grow. Think about the parents that never got to watch their baby girl take her first step or their baby boy say his first word. Unfortunately, a parent somewhere experiences that very scenario due to child mortality.

By definition child mortality is the death of children under the age of five. While the causes may vary, many children die soon after birth from cases such as, pneumonia, childbirth complications, diarrhea, malaria, and HIV. Studies show that in 2013 alone there were more than 6.3 million child deaths under the age five (World Health Organization).

There are times where such mortality is inevitable, but in the same sense there are just as many times where such mortality can be prevented.

About 45% of all child deaths are linked to malnutrition; these are cases where children lack sufficient nutrients in their body. In 2013 alone roughly 17,000 children died each day. According to the UN's Standing Committee on Nutrition, "Malnutrition is the largest single contributor to disease in the world." In many countries, the necessities taken for granted here in the United States are scarce. There are programs set in place to reduce child mortality, such as UNICEF that actively reduces child mortality around the world.

According to UNICEF, "the program was created with a distinct purpose in mind: to work with others to overcome the obstacles that poverty, violence, disease and discrimination place in a child's path." The program was created after World War II by the United Nations to provide food, clothing and health care to children and their families that faced famine and disease. The program has focused on sustaining the quality and quantity of food a person eats and ensures adequate health care and a healthy environment.

The UNICEF Program set a goal to decrease the child mortality rate from 93 children in every 1000 (1990 rate) to 31 children in every 1000 by 2016. To accomplish this goal the program has set in place aids to raise awareness. Donations will allow the program to provide vaccination shots and vitamins, water purification tablets for healthier eating and drinking, and further research to prevent diseases. There are thousands of ways that we can make this world a better place, but it has to start somewhere. It has to start with you; you can make a difference. You can save a life.

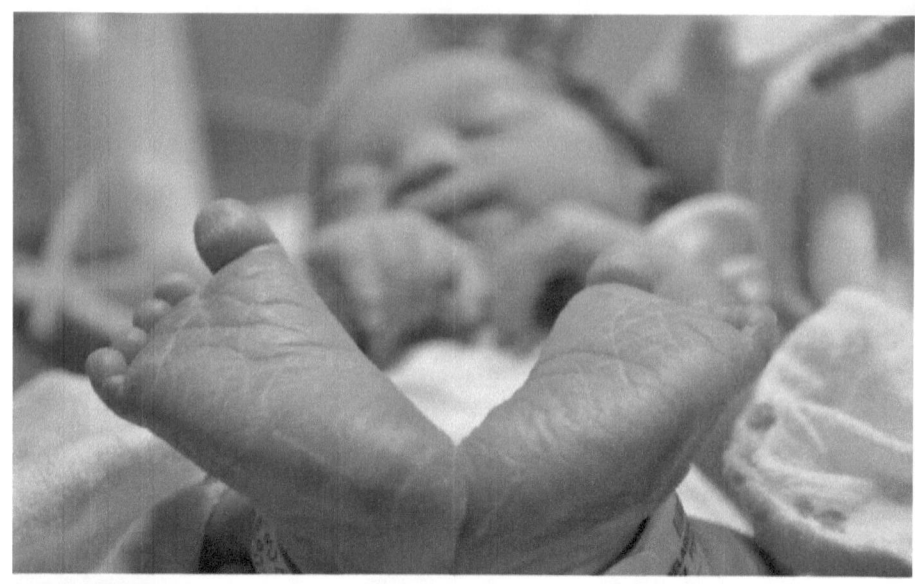

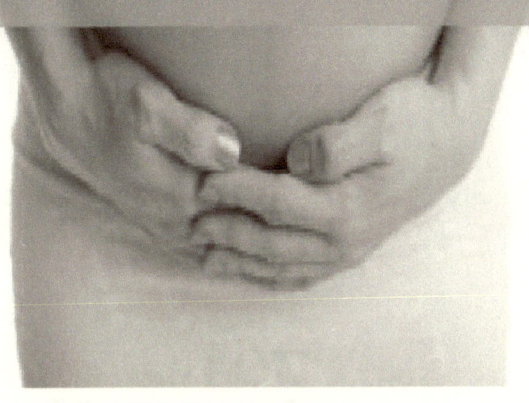

GOAL 5

Improve Maternal Health

Rachel Dalton *has a Bachelors of Science in Psychology and Political Science from Roosevelt University. She is currently working on her M.B.A with concentrations in health services administration and economics from Roosevelt University. She is a member of the United Nations Association of Greater Chicago, as well as a member of the Roosevelt University UNA-USA Student Chapter. She has extensive experience in children and adolescent*  *mental health, as well as quality improvement and program evaluation. Her goal is to eventually receive a doctorate in public health and continue to champion international reproductive health. The MDG (Millennial Development Goal) that stood out to her was **#5 Improving Maternal Health!***

Improve Maternal Health

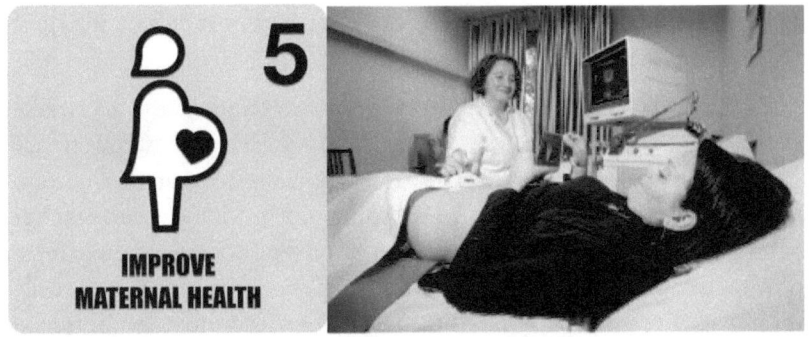

IMPROVE MATERNAL HEALTH

In the year 2000, the United Nations created the eight Millennium Development Goals at the Millennium Summit, where one hundred and eighty nine countries and twenty-three international organizations declared their commitment to achieving these goals by 2015. Millennium Goal Five aims to improve maternal health by reducing the maternal mortality ratio by three quarters and achieving universal access to reproductive health. There has been great progress towards MDG 5, but the global community still needs to do more if this goal is going to be attained.

Investing in reproductive health is vital to improving the economies of the developing world and the developed world. Even in the United States, universal access to reproductive health services is lacking. What would be the impact of universal access to reproductive health? What are the benefits?

Per the Post-2015 Consensus research project at the Copenhagen Consensus Center, providing reproductive services to all persons who want them will cost $3.6 billion a year, but will generate benefits of up to $432 billion a year. There is a negative correlation between access to contraception and maternal deaths. If the unmet need for family planning was met in the developing world, then the lives of so many women and babies would be saved. Investment in contraceptive services, not only saves lives, but saves money by preventing costly healthcare spending on unintended pregnancies. If women are given the opportunity to space their pregnancies and control the number of children they have, then they would be able to contribute more to the economy. Young girls would be able to stay in school longer. Educated women become skilled workers, who contribute to the economy not only with their skills, but also with their purchasing power.

Women need to feel confident in the ability to make decisions on their reproductive health. Too many women are influenced by partners and religious authorities to not use certain methods of contraception. According to a 2014 Guttmacher Institute study, women are not educated enough on the side effects and effectiveness of various methods of contraception. Family planning services not only need to be far reaching, but also better at educating women on contraceptive methods.

The United Nation Foundation's Universal Access Project has championed universal access to reproductive health by encouraging policymakers in donor governments, including the United States, to invest in international reproductive health and family planning. The Universal Access Project started in 2008, and since then, the initiative increased U.S spending on international reproductive health by thirty percent and has reinstated U.S funding for the United Nations Population Fund. There is an unmet need for reproductive health services for over 220 million women worldwide. Thankfully organizations like the United Nations Foundation, UNFPA, and the Guttmacher Institute are championing reproductive health, and by doing so, these organizations are not only helping to achieve Millennium Development Goal 5, but also are helping women all over the world reach their full potential.

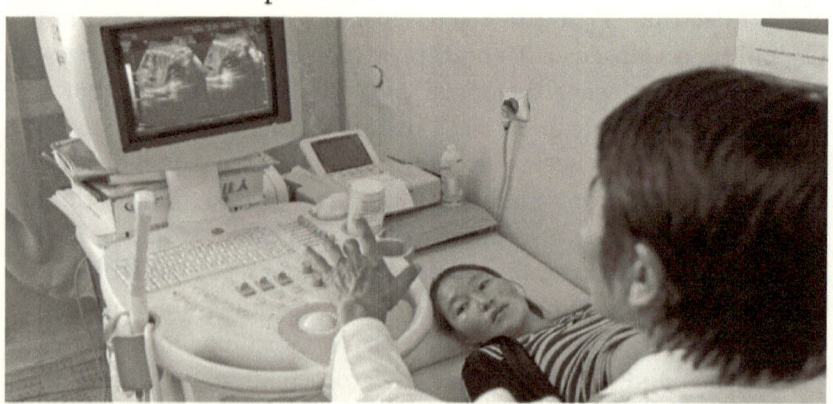

GOAL
6
FORUM
MDG6
Combat HIV/AIDS, Malaria and Other Diseases

Blessing JaJa is the President of Robert Morris University UNA USA Student Chapter. She is currently an undergrad student at Robert Morris University of Illinois pursuing a business degree. When asked why she joined the United Nations Association's Student Chapter her response was, "for personal reasons, after being part of Interact Club my entire high school career I became aware of world problems. We focused on health and this made the UNA USA Student Chapter a great way for me to continue helping while I am in Collage!"

Combat HIV/AIDs Malaria and Other Diseases

COMBAT HIV/AIDS, MALARIA AND OTHER DISEASES

Africa, the beginning of life. A land filled with so much resources like oil, gold, diamonds, iron, silver and cocoa beans. Unfortunately, the living conditions of many people living in this continent are beyond poor. This is due to corrupt government rulings, weakened court system and carelessness. The governments in some parts of Africa fail to protect its citizens, especially the women. Corruption has become deeply entrenched in some parts of Africa, part of what spreads corruption in the countries is the lack of information, the lack of punishment for crime and the government failed attempts to help their own country.

As a West African native, growing up I would see my parents filling up barrels with medicine to send back to Africa. My aunt owned a clinic and would treat all of the women with HIV, most of them were pregnant. When she would ask them how it happened the women would say they were raped. Many people think the reason why HIV cases are increasing in Africa is because the natives are not aware of the deadly disease and are not taught sexual education. When in all actuality the reason why the cases are increasing is due to rape. Rape is such a common crime in some parts of Africa it's sickening, men that know they have this disease repeatedly rape defenseless women. But because the government does not protect women rights and the court system is corrupt the men do not get punished, and because of that they continue to rape and infect multiple women.

I believe apart from people's lack of awareness as how to protect themselves, there is a greater sense of carelessness because of the fact that no punishment exists. If the government protected women and men were punished for their crime, the cases of HIV and rape along with other crimes would dramatically drop. But because the men know that they will not be punished they continue to endanger women. In order to combat diseases like HIV, we need to target the root. There is a reason the cases are still increasing, even after sex - education is taught, and that is the government. The government is responsible for its citizen's protection, but because it fails to protect, the problem continues to rise.

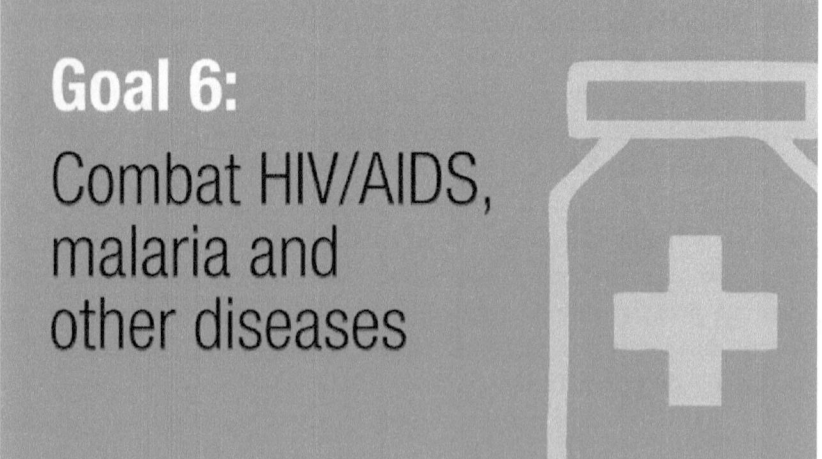

Goal 6:

Combat HIV/AIDS, malaria and other diseases

HIV/AIDs is a global pandemic. 2.1 million people worldwide became newly affected in 2013, according to the World Health Organization (WHO). There isn't a country that has not somehow been affected by HIV/AIDs. Yet, at the local level, it appears to have been under the radar. Some people were jostled by the recent news of an HIV outbreak in the state of Indiana. Many who are not among the "at risk group" have had little to no discussions about HIV/AIDs in recent years and the topic rarely comes up in the media. Its absence in the public discourse has led to a false sense that HIV /AIDs is no longer an issue of national concern. The outbreak in Indiana led me to wonder where the US stood in its global commitment to eradicating this disease. Although the vast majority of individuals living with the HIV virus are in low and middle income countries, I discovered that one million people in the U.S. are living with HIV and one in seven is unaware of their infection. What surprised and concerned me the most was that one in four new HIV infections is among youths ages 13-24 and only 49% of youth living with HIV have been diagnosed (aids.gov).

I have children in that age range, I thought. Suddenly, the topic had a renewed sense of urgency for me. I wondered if my children ever thought about the topic or even discussed it with their friends. It has not been a topic of conversation at our house. It probably isn't a topic at their friends' house either. So, I asked myself, how would they know how to protect themselves? How would they know that some of the new HIV infections are among youths their age, some of whom are not even aware they are infected? They probably don't know. Youth education on this matter is important. They need to know that approximately 50,000 people become infected each year. They need to know that, according to the Center of Diseases Control, the new cases of HIV infections in 2010, were: 63% MSM, 25% Heterosexuals, 8% injection drug users (IDU), and 3% IUD-MSM. They need to know that HIV/AID is not a nonchalant matter. Who should inform them? Well, the education should begin at home and continue in the schools. At some point, it should become part of their casual conversations with friends. Technology presents an opportunity on that front. Social media and mobile apps are popular among this generation of youth. Why not use these tools as platforms to engage and informed them, whether it be through targeted information ads or mobile app games. The more individuals that are educated on this topic the greater our chances for eradicating this disease.

The story on HIV/AID is a series of good news and bad news. For example, the good news is that in the US, there is only four estimated transmission of HIV per year for every 100 people living with HIV (CDC). In 2011, 86% of people living with HIV knew their diagnosis compared to 80.9 in 2006 (whitehouse.gov). The bad news is approximately 50,000 people become infected each year. The key challenges cited by a CDC report are (1) the increasing numbers of new infections among gay, bisexual and other men who have sex with men (MSM) and (2) racial and ethnic disparities in access to care and treatment. The outbreak in Indiana was an eye opener. It became apparent that more is needed with regard to HIV testing and education in the U.S. We must focus our resources on the most at risk populations (sex workers, IDUs, etc...), in light of the fact that the outbreak in Indiana was attributed to injection drug users (IDU). HIV/AIDs must remain on the radar until we can report better outcomes than those cited above.

Dr. Monique Herard

GOAL 7

Ensure Environmental Sustainability

Mary Lorraine Andoh is *a member of the Student UNA-USA Roosevelt University Chapter. She is 23-year-old graduate student studying public administration, with an emphasis in health care services. She has a keen interest in expanding education and healthcare access for children from all economic backgrounds. Since returning from a three-month internship with the World Education Organization in Accra, Ghana, she is extremely excited to be at Roosevelt University and looks forward to the upcoming year as a new member of UNA.*

*The Goal that impacted her the most as a Student Member of the Roosevelt University's UNA-USA is **#7 Ensure Environmental Sustainability.***

ENSURE ENVIRONMENTAL SUSTAINABILITY

ENSURE ENVIRONMENTAL SUSTAINABILITY

The United Nations Millennium goals were established to encourage peace and a cohesive global economy by addressing the most important issues that are being faced in the world today. A lot of attention is given to combating diseases, and ending world hunger, but those are not the only issues that we have to invest in, in order to reach the millennium goals. Education and health will always be the foundation that needs in place in order for us to move forward, but we need to focus on **Environmental Sustainability** in order to have a lasting effect.

We cannot just create solutions and not teach our communities how to use those tools. Eradicating poverty and hunger will not go away by delivering food to children who are hungry. We need to be in those communities, working governments on how to capitalize on the resources that are there. Whether it is teaching a small community how to grow food, or even encouraging citizens to buy homegrown goods and food, all can make a difference in helping an economy and strengthening the belief that as a people, we really can help ourselves.

Achieving universal primary education and increasing the role of women in education is also very critical. The education of women is an overlooked and undeveloped but very powerful tool. Yes, the right to schooling is important for everyone, but it holds a special significance for women.

For example, according to the United Nations Educational, Scientific, and Cultural Organization (UNESCO) found women who at least reach a primary school education are 13 percent more likely to know that a condom can reduce their risk of contracting HIV/AIDS. In the "traditional" family role, women are usually seen to have a greater influence in household matters and can empower them to make healthier decisions for themselves, their families and future generations. Though we should pay a little more attention to some of these goals, by no means is one goal more important than the other. Making strides in all areas means that we as a generation are taking the initiatives towards not only a healthy global lifestyle, but also a prosperous future.

Photo Credit/Crédit photographique: Dan Crosbie

GOAL 8

Global Partnership for
Development

Eric Kelley *is a member of the Student UNA-USA Roosevelt University Chapter. He received his Bachelor of Arts in Political Science from Ohio State University and has recently graduated with his Master of Public Administration from Roosevelt University. He has a bevy of political experience previously working in Congressman Tim Ryan's office (OH- 13th District), Roosevelt University's Community & Government Relations Office, and on multiple campaigns and is currently a member of the United Nations Association- Chicago. He is an ardent supporter of human rights and justice. Despite being a life-long Cleveland fan, he also maintains a passion for sports.*

*Being a member of the UNA-USA student Chapter has changed his life. It has given him a chance to help make a change in a world where people don't realize it only takes one person at a time to see change! The UNA Millennial Goal that stood out for him was **#8 A Global Partnerships for Development.***

A Global Partnership for Development- Realizing the Goal

GLOBAL
PARTNERSHIP FOR
DEVELOPMENT

With a 24 hour news cycle rife with coverage of war, economic disparity, and disaster- a Global Partnership for Development (GPD) may sound quixotic: Citizens of the world working in tandem, altruistically, towards a common goal. But in reality, this work takes place on a daily basis. In 2013 alone, $134.8 billion was committed to official development assistance. Accordingly, the United Nation's Millennium Development Goal (MDG) 8: Developing a Global Partnership for Development has lofty expectations, but will also produce resonating results.

Auspiciously, that number is an increase from 2012 and 2013, when many countries took austerity measures, to an all-time high in aid.1 However, with only five countries of the 28 country Development Assistance Council meeting the United Nations' target of a 0.7% ratio of Official Development Assistance to Gross National Income, much work is still to be done.

Although 0.7% may seem like a meager target, it is an attainable goal which can affect real change in the world. For example, Austria was able to commit .28% of Official Development Assistance as a percent of their Gross National Income, but that equated to USD $1.17 billion in aid.1 The neediest parts of the world, such as sub-Saharan African, depend upon this type of aid, and would be certainly worse off without it.

Not only are governments responsible for a Global Partnership for Development, but private entities as well. To this end, the United Nations specifically created sub-targets in its GPD to encourage the private investment community (Targets 8E & 8F). As such, the World Bank and UNDP have focused on poverty-centered and employment creation which must be merged into private sector development. This must occur by social participatory approaches appreciating the productive entitlement and empowerment of the marginalized populations in a social market economy. Therefore, it is imperative for private companies, such as pharmaceutical companies, to realize the importance and ethical prominence of their developmental efforts.

Furthermore, as technology evolves and makes information and communication more accessible, it is crucial that companies take the initiative. As then Secretary of State Hillary Clinton stated, "Innovation, science, and technology must again become fundamental components of how we conduct development work and the only way we can do that is with your help."4 Companies, like Microsoft's $940 million (fair market value, FY14) in software donations worldwide, will continue to make the vast amount of online resources, worldwide connectivity, and information more readily available to the people who can use those most.

Advocating for a Global Partnership can and will be a foundation to expanding and advancing the United Nation's seven remaining Millennium goals. Cementing more and more entities into this network of committed partners will provide not only money, but also exposure, physical resources, and access to individuals dedicated to progressing the Millennium Development Goals agenda.

The United Nation's eighth MDG of developing a Global Partnership for Development is ambitious in the least; but it is certainly not unrealistic. These partnerships occur every day and must only be nurtured and advanced to begin to meet the expectations of MDG number eight. A Global Partnership for Development aims high to perpetuate the understanding of the worldwide developmental needs while reinforcing the remaining seven goals.

A brief history and analysis of the United Nations Millennial and Sustainable Developmental Goals.

By Dr. La Vonne Downey

The momentum of the ideas of a select group of experts who working on issues of global poverty, which expanded to include the voices of people living with the issues, governments, and nongovernmental actors all working together towards a set of measurable goals, sums up the history of the United Nations Millennium Development Goals (MDG). The process germinated through specialized summits where target interest groups raised and reported on a series of specific issues that emerged on a global scale (Bradford, 2006). This disparate collection of global problems and solutions resulted in the United Nations Secretary General commissioning of a report that would tie together the most important world development issues. The result was a global agreement to reduce, through comprehensive and collaborative actions, world poverty and human deprivation. They were different in part due to their scope which focused on eight goals and to their global commitment and promise to initiate, implement, support, and monitor their progress.

This was not the first time in history such a global undertaking to improve the health and wealth of the world's global citizen had taken place. It was instead an outcome of a multiple decades long waxing and waning global policy driven by multiply actors. The germination of the MDG can be seen as far back as when in January 1941 when the United States (U.S). President Franklin D. Roosevelt spoke about the "Four Freedoms" which included the freedom from want and fear (Toye, 2005).

Also, in the Declaration of Human Rights in 1948, that referred to individuals having the right to a standard of living adequate for health and well being of him/her self and their family. The 1960's and 1970's saw many governments make such proclamations often without subsequent support or monitoring of specific measurable goals (Toye, 2005). During this time period aid to developing nations was often tied to alignment building in the ongoing Cold War between the U.S.S.R and the U.S. The 1980's saw the rise of newer nongovernmental actors such as the International Monetary Fund and the World Bank. Their approach was different in that it focused on the role of economic markets. This meant its focus was on liberalization and privatization of economic markets as well as a reduction in the role of governments. This often had disastrous impact for developing countries such as those in Latin American who experienced numerous economic crises (Brown, 2002, Reinicke, 1998). Africa also was impacted by this new approach resulted in a range of negative outcomes such as a generation of stagnation with rising poverty, raising child deaths, and drops in life expectancy. For these reasons that period is now referred to as development's 'lost decade (Hume, 2009).

The increase in poverty despite market driven approaches was noted in the first of its kind World Bank World Development Report 1990. This report, in addition to the Human Development report from the United Nations Development Program started to put poverty and poverty reduction back on the policy map (Eyben, 2006, IMF, 2000). Together they helped to move the discussion away from talking about the means through economic growth to include how these means would impact people's lives (Peterson, 2006).

This change in singular approach and direction about poverty started a decade's long series of UN summits and meetings which included: the world conference on education, the Children's Conference, the Rio Climate Summit, Human Rights Conference, Cairo Conference on Populations and Development, World Conference on Social Development, and the Beijing Women's Conference. These conferences served to generate a list of issues and concerns that impacted the global community; however the resources to do something about these issues did not exist as globally monies for development was declining (Toye, 2005, Clemens 2004, Stone, 2008). This was in part due to the new political climate after the end of the Cold War. Nations felt less of a need to use global development funds to support or generate allies in poor non aligned countries and instead used these monies to reduce donor countries debt and improve their own social programs (Emmeriji, 2001).

Despite this reduction the conversation about global issues and how to deal with them continued. The problem was that this was being carried out by rich nation states whose focus often did not include the priorities of the United Nations and its agencies, and, of nongovernmental actors such as IMF. Thus a two focus approach was being seen, one focused on human rights definition and enabling those rights approach and a market approach which had measurable markers of success (Eyben, 2006, Bradford 2002).

This two track approach continued into the late 1990's with various countries taking the lead. As a response to this uptick in global poverty awareness the United Nation and it Secretary General Kofi Annan planned for a Millennium event (MacArthur, 2013). This was to be a large and inclusive summit to create a space for the key issues of global poverty to come together and generate a plan of action.

Thus on April 2000 Kofi Annan issued the We the People: The Role of the United Nations in the 21st Century report. This document was to set the agenda for the upcoming Millennium summit with poverty eradication as the most import global issue (Annan, 2000). This set off a year long negotiations between special interest groups, nation states, the UN and it agencies, and nongovernmental actors. Even well into 2001 groups such as a task force from the UN, World Bank, and the International Monetary Fund had ongoing negotiations in order to produce the final list of Millennium Development Goals we now know of today. The negotiations that produced the MDG's varied greatly between different individuals, groups, organizations, states and or groups of states. (Sinding, 2004, Standing, 200, Sen 2005)

Once they were presented to the UN General Assembly the MDG set up a framework that could be used as a rallying point for governments, nongovernmental actors and the UN to use for a call to action (see appendix 1). Those differing sets of actors also were able to bring together experts from academia, business, government, and civil-society to build a plan of action to achieve these goals. There were also a range of individuals and organizations that became cheerleaders for the goals. They included: developing countries, and various NGO leaders who encouraged civil-society leaders to hold their governments accountable for meeting the goals (Sach, 2005). In developed countries, organizations such as ONE.org fronted by activist Jamie Drummond and the rock star Bono, engaged in a worldwide public awareness campaign in addition to petitioning politicians to demand that world leaders make efforts to meet these new targets (Hume 2009).

The MDG's were not universally praised or followed. There were countries and nongovernmental actors that did not publically endorse the goals such as the World Bank and the United States. Both the U.S president Bush and the World Bank viewed them as UN dictating policy to which neither felt beholden (Easterly, 2006, Bradford, 2006, Clemens, 2007) However, despite this both lent types of support to the goals. The World Bank has increased its budget for the International Development Association, which gives economic and technical support to the world's poorest countries. In the case of the US it provided resources, such as Bush's AIDS initiative. Subsequently, nongovernmental actors such as the Gates Foundation focused efforts on malaria, worldwide immunizations and eradication of childhood diseases that helped revolutionize global health (Hume, 2009, MacArthur, 2013). Thus they were both the capital economically, technically and socially in meeting many of the central aspects of goals four and six.

The results so far are mixed and vary by region. As of 2010, five years prior to the 2015 deadline the world had met the goal of cutting extreme poverty by half (UN Millennium Development Goals Report 2014). In Africa there has been an unprecedented economic growth and poverty reductions. Prior to the MDG, poverty in sub-Saharan Africa rose from 52% to 58%. Since the goals however it has declined to 48% as of 2008, in part due to MDG backed investment which has resulted in healthier and more educated populations. The MDG also had an impact on food security which provided support for small and cash crop farms to reduce both hunger and poverty (UN Millennium Report 2014).

The level of primary education (goal two), has also increased globally, but especially in South Asia and sub-Saharan Africa. Again, this is due to global funding partnerships with such groups as the Global Partnership for Education and The World Bank, around MDG number two to achieve universal primary education (MacArthur, 2013). These nongovernmental actors have provided finance and guidance in terms of training and capacity building. This helped to close the gaps that existed in providing education to all including both genders to achieve gender parity in education (UN Millennium Report 2014).

The biggest impact, however, has been in achievement of (goal six): combating HIV/AIDS, Malaria and other diseases and subsequently goal four reducing child mortality. The MDG goals were able to provide a rallying call to numerous nongovernmental actors such as the GAVI alliance and the Gates foundation. These actors brought an increase not only in private financial aid but also a business model approach that focus on a continuous monitoring of performance, outcomes and results. In part due to their efforts despite an increase in global populations there has been a decrease in children dying before the age of five from 11.7 million in 1990 to 6.9 million in 2011 (MacArthur 2013). The treatment of HIV/AIDs has also seen an influx of governmental and nongovernmental support, increasing those receiving treatment for HIV/AIDs and to reducing the number of deaths. In 2000, nearly 30 million people were infected, the vast majority in Africa, and only 10,000 people were in treatment. This resulted in over one million people were dying every year from the disease. Progress has meant that by the end of 2011 eight million people were receiving treatment and the numbers of deaths were reduced by 70% (MacArthur, 2013, Hume, 2009, Economist 2015).

The progress on the MDG is not uniformly successful. Each goal as of 2014 has places where the objectives are not met. With regards to goal one (eradicating extreme poverty), sub-Sahara Africa has large deficits in the area of reduction of rate by half, production of employment and reduction of hunger. In goal three (promoting gender equality) there is still low amounts of women share of employment in Northern Africa, and in Western Southern Asia. In women's representation in national parliament there is low representation in South Eastern, Southern, and Western Asia, Oceania, and Central Asia. In goal 5(improve maternal health) sub Saharan Africa is still experiencing high mortality and low access to reproductive health. In goal 6 (combating HIV/AIDs, malaria and other diseases) sub Saharan Africa still have high incidences and mortality of HIV/AIDs and tuberculosis. Goal seven (ensuring environmental sustainability) there are has been an uneven progress on all targets with sub-Saharan Africa and Oceana have too few with access to drinking water. Additionally, Southern Asia, sub Saharan African and Oceana still having low levels of sanitation and those living in all of Africa, South Eastern and Southern Asia has high levels of slum dwellings (UN Millennium Report 2014).

Overall the MDG have shown that with an expansion of players who concentrate their efforts, the issues of global health and poverty can be addressed. However, there is still much to be done hence the proposed Sustainable Development Goals (SDG). These goals were the outcome of the Rio+20 Summit in 2012. The outcome which was presented to the UN general assembly in September of 2014 consisted of 17 goals (see appendix 2). They go beyond addressing poverty and the needs of the poor to deal with climate change, income inequality and infrastructure issues (MacArthur, 2013, Economist March 2015). Some countries have voiced support for the 17 goals, many of which contain the previous eight MDG but have expanded upon them in detail and in scope. Some of the member states and NGO.s however have stated they that they see the 17 SDG with a total of 168 targets as to big and complex to sell to the public (see appendix 3). The idea of less is better seems to be the consensus among many in the developed nation.

The second concern is who will be financially supporting these goals. The cost by some estimates is cost about $66billion a year, while annual investments in improving infrastructure (water, agriculture, transport, power) could be up to a total of $7trillion globally (MacArthur, 2013). This has prompted some countries to look at their cost effectiveness. The Copenhagen Consensus Centre has found that out of the 169 targets only eighteen would have a rate of return of $15 or more for every dollar spent. Out of the eighteen more than half of them focus on health interventions and public health issue. (Copenhagen Consensus Center Report 2015)

In order to build consensus around which of any of the 17 goals and 169 targets will remain the UN has created an information campaign. It is also engaging adding more voices to process thus its "global conversations" campaign which is asking people to comment and prioritize the goals. These will then become part of the UN working group's discussion prior to presenting the goals to the UN general assembly.

One thing is certain, based on the success of the previous 2015 goals there are aspects which should be duplicated. The next generation of goals needs to be accessible and simple. This has been part of the reasons for the previous 2015 goals success in that they were understandable and measurable. They also had flexibility in how they were done thus giving each country local variation in how they achieved the goals. It had accountability and determining outcomes which allowed for governments and nongovernmental organizations to tract success and to change directions if and when policies were not working to reduce and or met goals. The ability to focus on measurable outcomes was part of the 2015 goals ability to succeed and must be part of the next stage of the goal development. The 2015 MDG goals were able to provide a multi-dimensional understanding of global issues such as poverty and still be able to produce measurable standards with which to hold both governments and nongovernmental organizations accountable (Sachs, 2005, Stone, 2008, Clemens, 2007,). They were able to garner world support even in countries such as the U.S., where politicians did not fully support them. This was in part due to their ability to generate popular support from individuals and organizations from within those countries. The outcome is undeniable in that millions of lives have been impacted and saved due to the MDG 2015. It is a blueprint of what can be achieved when there is a bringing together of the best minds, best practices with accountability and transparency towards results coupled with resources from numerous individuals, organizations, and governments. They are a testament to what can be achieved when we go beyond ourselves, our countries and our government to truly engage in the world as a responsible, informed, caring global family.

Appendix 1 – The Millennium Development Goals

Goal 1: Eradicate extreme poverty and hunger

Target 1: Halve, between 1990 and 2015, the proportion of people whose income is less than one dollar a day.
Target 2: Halve, between 1990 and 2015, the proportion of people who suffer from hunger.

Goal 2: Achieve universal primary education
Target 3: Ensure that, by 2015, children everywhere, boys and girls alike, will be able to complete a full course of primary schooling.

Goal 3: Promote gender equality and empower women
Target 4: Eliminate gender disparity in primary and secondary education, preferably by
2005, and to all levels of education no later than 2015.

Goal 4: Reduce child mortality
Target 5: Reduce by two-thirds, between 1990 and 2015, the under-five mortality rate.

Goal 5: Improve maternal health
Target 6: Reduce by three-quarters, between 1990 and 2015, the maternal mortality ratio.

Goal 6: Combat HIV/AIDS, malaria and other diseases
Target 7: Have halted by 2015 and begun to reverse the spread of HIV/AIDS.
Target 8: Have halted by 2015 and begun to reverse the incidence of malaria and other major diseases.

Goal 7: Ensure environmental sustainability
Target 9: Integrate the principles of sustainable development into country policies and programmes and reverse the loss of environmental resources.

Target 10: Halve, by 2015, the proportion of people without sustainable access to safe drinking water.

Target 11: By 2020, to have achieved a significant improvement in the lives of at least 100 million slum dwellers.

Goal 8: Develop a global partnership for development

Target 12: Develop further an open, rule-based, predictable, non-discriminatory trading and financial system.

Target 13: Address the special needs of the least developed countries.

Target 14: Address the special needs of landlocked countries and small island developing states.

Target 15: Deal comprehensively with the debt problems of developing countries through national and international measures in order to make debt sustainable in the long term.

Target 16: In cooperation with developing countries, develop and implement strategies for decent and productive work for youth.

Target 17: In cooperation with pharmaceutical companies, provide access to affordable, essential drugs in developing countries.

Target 18: In cooperation with the private sector, make available the benefits of new technologies, especially information and communications.

Source
: UN (2001), pp. 56-58

Appendix 2 Sustainable Development Goals

Goal 1 End poverty in all its forms everywhere

Goal 2 End hunger, achieve food security and improved nutrition and promote sustainable agriculture

Goal 3 Ensure healthy lives and promote well-being for all at all ages

Goal 4 Ensure inclusive and equitable quality education and promote lifelong learning opportunities for all

Goal 5 Achieve gender equality and empower all women and girls

Goal 6 Ensure availability and sustainable management of water and sanitation for all

Goal 7 Ensure access to affordable, reliable, sustainable and modern energy for all

Goal 8 Promote sustained, inclusive and sustainable economic growth, full and productive employment and decent work for all

Goal 9 Build resilient infrastructure, promote inclusive and sustainable industrialization and foster innovation

Goal 10 Reduce inequality within and among countries

Goal 11 Make cities and human settlements inclusive, safe, resilient and sustainable

Goal 12 Ensure sustainable consumption and production patterns

Goal 13 Take urgent action to combat climate change and its impacts*

Goal 14 Conserve and sustainably use the oceans, seas and marine resources for sustainable development

Goal 15 Protect, restore and promote sustainable use of terrestrial ecosystems, sustainably manage forests, combat desertification, and halt and reverse land degradation and halt biodiversity loss

Goal 16 Promote peaceful and inclusive societies for sustainable development, provide access to justice for all and build effective, accountable and inclusive institutions at all levels

Goal 17 Strengthen the means of implementation and revitalize the global partnership for sustainable development

Acknowledging that the United Nations Framework Convention on Climate Change is the primary international, intergovernmental forum for negotiating the global response to climate change

References

1. Aids.gov. *What is HIV/AIDs?* Retrieved May 1, 2015 from https://www.aids.gov/hiv-aids-basics/hiv-aids-101/statistics/index.html.

2. Annan, K. A. (2000). *We the Peoples: The Role of the United Nations in the 21st Century*. New York: United Nations Department of Public Information.

3. Bradford, C. (2002). *Towards 2015: From Consensus Formation to Implementation of the MDGs – The Historical Background, 1990-2002*. Mimeo. Washington, DC: The Brookings Institute.

4. Bradford, C. (2006). *History of the MDGs: A Personal Reflection*. Mimeo. Washington, DC: The Brookings Institute.

5. British Philosopher Herbert Spencer popular quote. Retrieved March 18, 2015 from http://www.gurteen.com/gurteen/gurteen.nsf/id/great-aim-of-education.

6. Brown, G. (2002). *Tackling Poverty: A Global New Deal – A Modern Marshall Plan for the Developing World*. London: HM

7. Center of Diseases Control – Division of HIV/AIDS Prevention. (2013). *Turning the Tide on HIV, Annual Report*. Retrieved May 1, 2015 from http://www.cdc.gov/hiv/pdf/policies_DHAP_AnnualReport2013.pdf.

8. Clemens, M. A. (2004). 'The Long Walk to School: International education goals in historical perspective'. Centre for Global Development Working Paper No. 37, Washington DC: Centre for Global Development.

9. Clemens, M. A., Kenny, C. J. and Moss, T. J. (2007). '*The trouble with the MDGs: Confronting expectations of aid and development success'.* World Development *35*(5), 735-751.

10. Copenhagen Censuses Report *Impact of Sustainable Goals 2015.* Retrieved March 2015 from http://www.copenhagenconsensus.com/

11. Corporate Citizenship- Technology for Good. Microsoft. Retrieved March 21, 2015 from http://www.microsoft.com/about/corporatecitizenship/en -us/nonprofits/

12. Dept. of State Press Release, July 8, 2010

13. Easterly, W. R. (2006). *The White Man's Burden: Why the West's Efforts to Aid the Rest Have Done So Much Ill and So Little Good.* Oxford: Oxford University Press.

14. Emmerij, L., Jolly, R. and Weiss, T. G. (2001). *Ahead of the Curve? UN Ideas and Global Challenges.* Bloomington, IN: Indiana University Press.

15. Eyben, R. (2006). 'The road not taken: International aid's choice of Copenhagen over Beijing'. *Third World Quarterly 27*(4), 595-608.

16. Fukofuka, S. (2009). "Foreign Aid Effectiveness: Fact or Fiction?" International Forum 12.2: 24-42. Print.

17. Hume David, (2009). The Millennium Development Goals (MDGs): A Short History of the World's Biggest Promise. University of Manchester-Institute for Development Policy and Management

18. IMF, OECD, UN and World Bank (2000). *A Better World For All: Progress towards the International Development Goals.* Washington, DC: IMF, OECD, UN and World Bank.

19. McAuthur, J. (2013). *Owning the Goals-What the Millennium Goals Have Accomplished.* Foreign Affairs, February 2013.

20. Millennium Development Goals: 2014 Progress Chart (2014). Retrieved March 27, 2015, from http://mdgs.un.org/unsd/mdg/Resources/Static/Products /Progress2014/Progress_E.pdf

21. Office of National AIDS Policy. (2014, December). *National HIV/AIDs Strategy.* Retrieved May 1, 2015 from https://www.whitehouse.gov/sites/default/files/docs/nha s_2014_progress_report_final_2.pdf

22. Organization for Economic Co-operation and Development. *Aid to developing countries rebounds in 2013 to reach an all-time high.* Retrieved March 21, 2015 from http://www.oecd.org/newsroom/aid-to-developing-countries-rebounds-in-2013-to-reach-an-all-time-high.htm

23. Pegg, D. (2013). 25 Compelling reasons why education is important. *List25*, Retrieved March 27, 2015, from http://list25.com/25-compelling-reasons-why-education-is-important/4/

24. Peterson, M. J. (2006). *The UN General Assembly.* London: Routledge.

25. Reinicke, W. H. (1998). *Global Public Policy: Governing Without Government?* Washington, DC: Brookings Institution Press.

26. Sachs, J. D. (2005). *The End of Poverty: Economic Possibilities for Our Time.* New York: Penguin Press.

27. Sachs, J. D. and McArthur, J. W. (2005). *'The Millennium Project: A plan for meeting the Millennium Development Goals'*. The Lancet 365(9456), 347-353.

28. Saith, A. (2006). *'From universal values to millennium development goals: Lost in translation'*. Development and Change 37(6), 1167-1199.

29. Sen, G. (2005). *'Gender equality and human rights: ICPD as a catalyst?'* In UNFPA (Ed.), The ICPD Vision: How Far has the 11-Year Journey taken Us? New York: United Nations Population Fund.

30. Silvia, B. and Choudhury, M. A. (2006). *A phenomenological conception of private sector responsibility in socioeconomic development"* International Journal of Social Economics 33(12), 796-807.

31. Sinding, S. W. (2004). *Address to the Symposium on the Millennium Development Goals and Sexual and Reproductive Health*, 30 November 2004, Rio de Janeiro (cited in B Crossette, 2004: 14).

32. Standing, H. (2004). *'Towards reproductive health for all?'* In R. Black and H. White (Eds.), Targeting Development: Critical Perspectives on the Millennium Development Goals (pp. 235-255). London: Routledge.

33. Stone, D. (2008). *'Global public policy, Transnational policy communities, and their networks'*. Policy Studies Journal 36(1), 19-38. The Economist. March 28th 2015. 14, 63-64.

34. Toye, J. and Toye, R. (2005a). *'From multilateralism to modernization: US strategy on trade, finance and development in the United Nations, 1945-63'*. Forum for Development Studies. 1, 127-150.

35. Toye, J. and Toye, R. (2005b). *'From new era to neo-liberalism: US strategy on trade, finance and development in the United Nations, 1964-82'*. Forum for Development Studies 1, 151-180.

36. Treasury.Schechter, M. G. (2005). United Nations Global Conferences. London: Routledge.

37. United Nations We Can End Poverty: Millennium Development Goals and Beyond 2015 Fact Sheet. Retrieved March 18, 2015 from http://www.un.org/millenniumgoals/pdf/Goal_2_fs.pdf.

38. UN (2001). *Road Map Towards the Implementation of the United Nations Millennium* Declaration: Report of the Secretary-General. New York: UN.

39. UN Millennium Project (2005). *Investing in Development: A Practical Plan to Achieve the Millennium Development Goals.* New York: Earthscan. UN The Millennium Development Goals Report 2014 at http://www.endpoverty2015.org/en/2014/07/07/the-millennium-development-goals-report-2014/accessed March 2015.

40. The Guarding (2015, Feb. 27). *Women are better off today, but still far from being equal with men.* Retrieved April 20, 2015 from http://www.theguardian.com/sponsored-content

41. World Food Programme (WFP.org). Food Keeps Girls in School in Yemen. Retrieved March 18, 2015 from http://www.wfp.org/stories/food-gets-girls-school-yemen.

42. World Health Organization. *HIV/AIDS Key Facts.* Retrieved May 1, 2015 from http://www.who.int/mediacentre/factsheets/fs360/en/

43. Yen, H. (2013). *4.1 Million Single-Mother Families Are Living In Poverty: Census*, Huffington Post, Retrieved April 20, 2015 from http://www.huffingtonpost.com/2013/09/19/single-mother-poverty_n_3953047.html

IMAGE CREDITS

1. United Nations Association, UNA-USA unausa.org
2. Agape Ministry located in Kakinda India
3. MDSterlingchic.com, Kimberly L.P. Wilson
4. UNA in Ghana
5. UNA in Mexico
6. Wikipedia

Index

www.ingramcontent.com/pod-product-compliance
Lightning Source LLC
Chambersburg PA
CBHW022123170526
45157CB00004B/1735